# Pandora

## Three Piano Duets
## by Naoko Ikeda

ISBN 1-4234-0735-0

WILLIS MUSIC

EXCLUSIVELY DISTRIBUTED BY

In Australia contact:
**Hal Leonard Australia Pty. Ltd.**
4 Lentara Court
Cheltenham, Victoria, 3192 Australia
Email: ausadmin@halleonard.com

Visit Hal Leonard Online at
**www.halleonard.com**

*To my friend, Mitsue*

# I. Song

## Secondo

Naoko Ikeda

Andante

con pedale

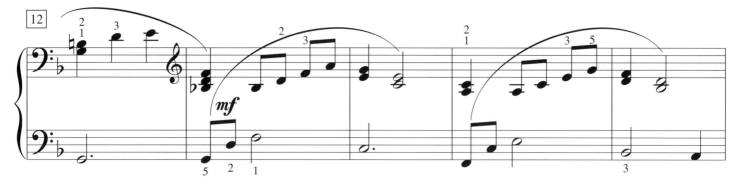

*To my friend, Mitsue*

# I. Song

### Primo

Naoko Ikeda

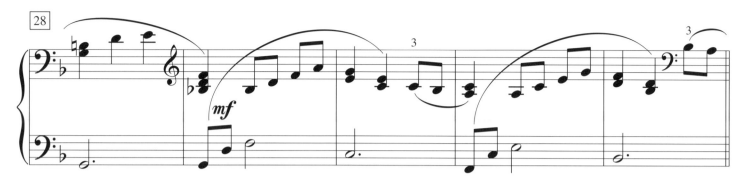

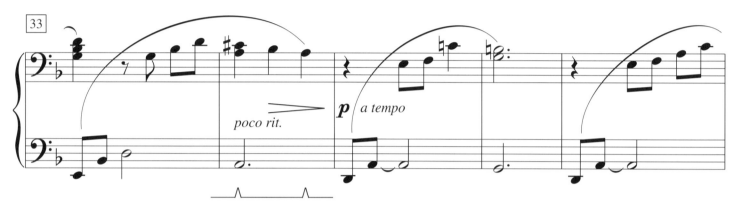

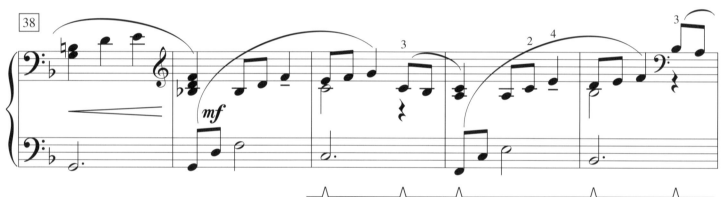

*To my friend, Michiyo*

# II. Dance
## Secondo

Naoko Ikeda

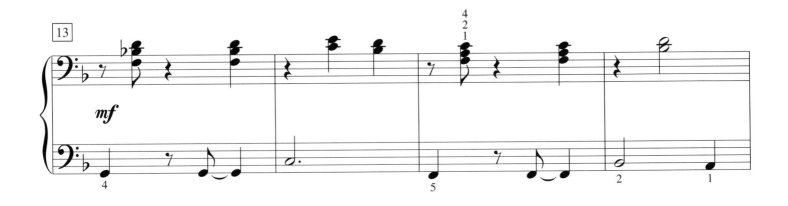

*To my friend, Michiyo*

# II. Dance

Primo

Naoko Ikeda

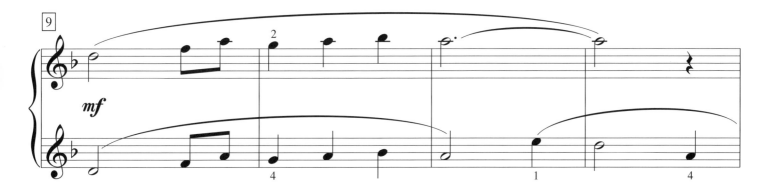

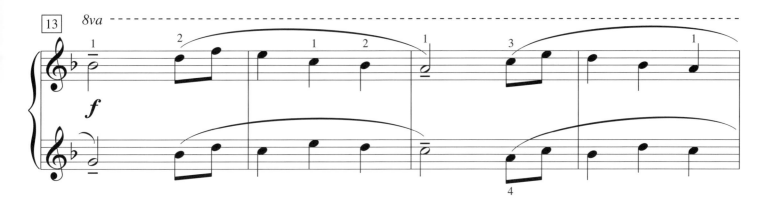

8

Secondo

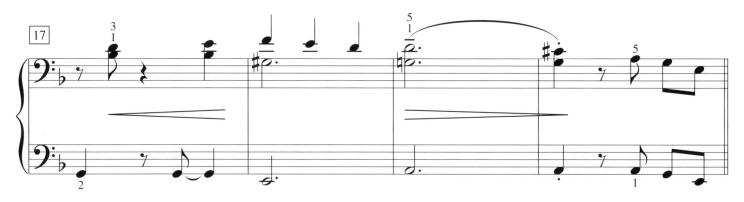

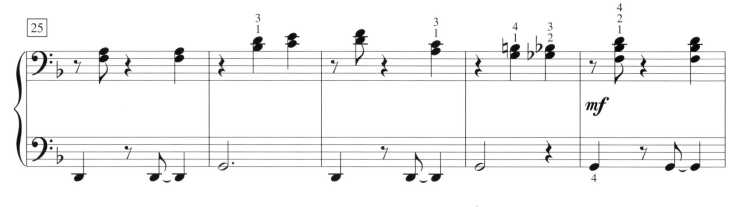

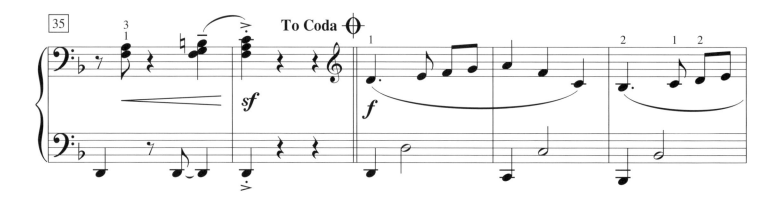

Primo

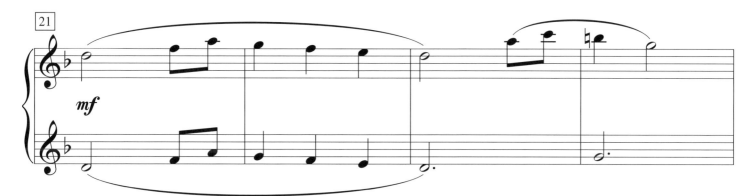

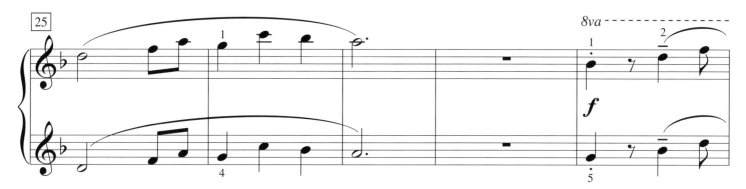

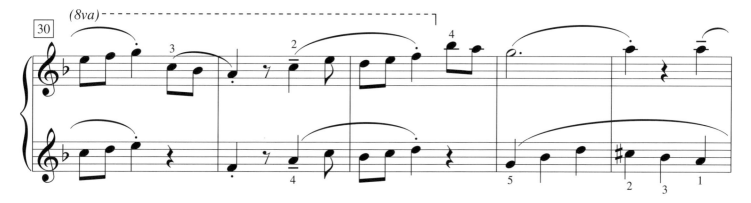

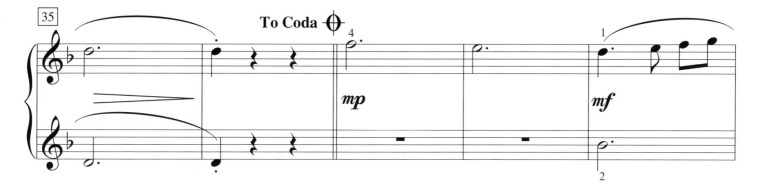

Secondo

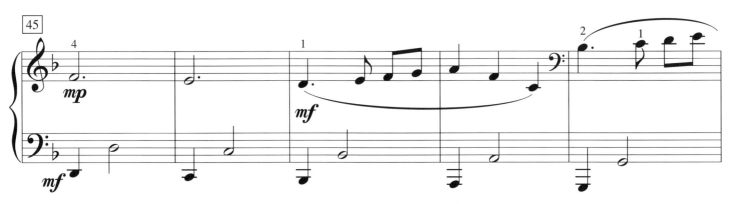

**D.S. al Coda**

**CODA**

*meno mosso*

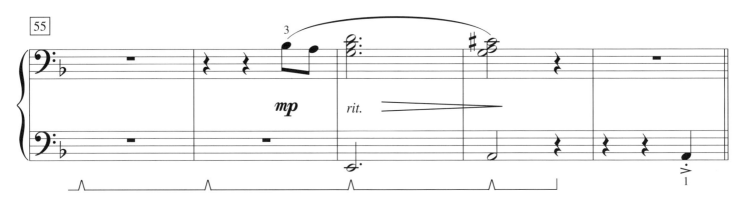

Primo

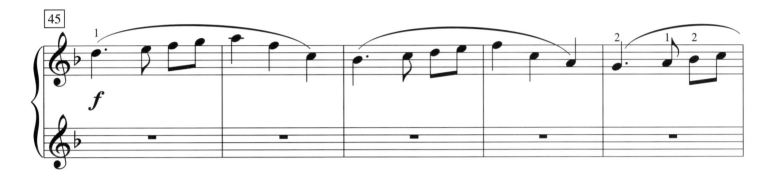

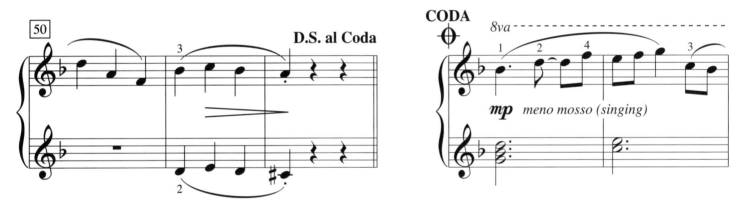

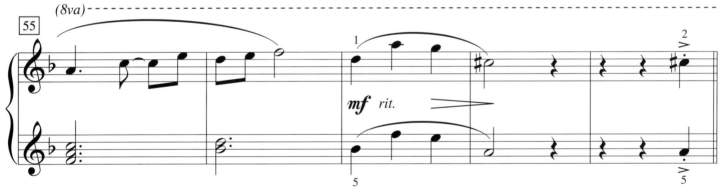

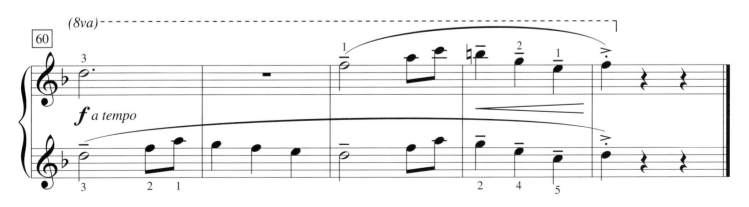

*To my friend, Sachiko*

# III. Hope

## Secondo

Naoko Ikeda

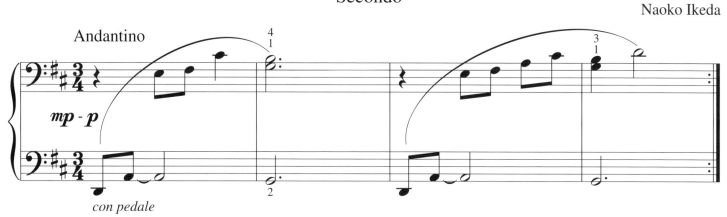

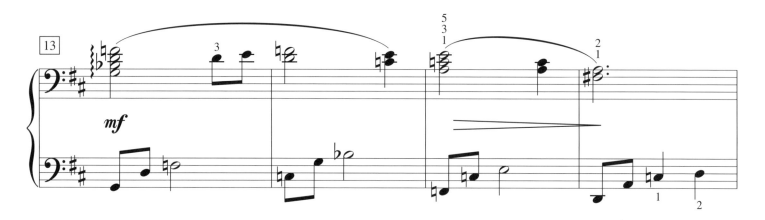

*To my friend, Sachiko*

# III. Hope

## Primo

Naoko Ikeda

Andantino

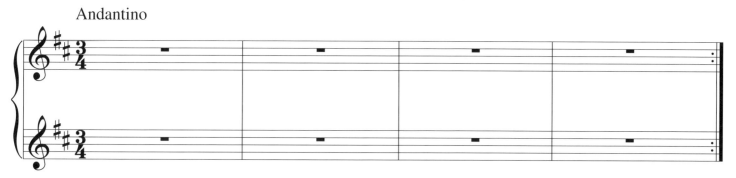

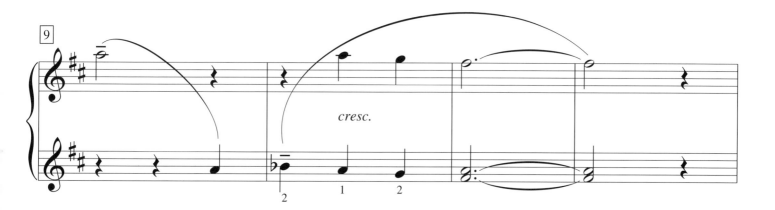

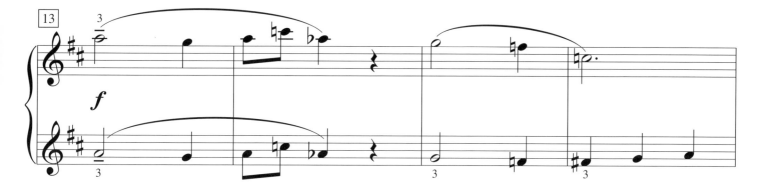

# Secondo

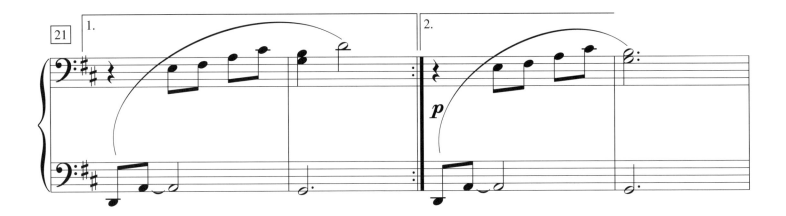

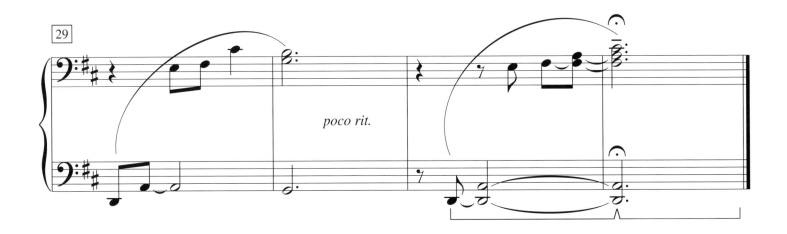

Primo